AnimalWays

Elephants

AnimalWays

Elephants

GLORIA G. SCHLAEPFER

BENCHMARK BOOKS

MARSHALL CAVENDISH
NEW YORK

With thanks to Dr. Dan Wharton, director of the Central Park Wildlife Center, for his expert reading of this manuscript.

Benchmark Books
Marshall Cavendish
99 White Plains Road
Tarrytown, NY 10591-9001
Web Site: www.marshallcavendish.com

Library of Congress Cataloging-in-Publication Data
Schlaepfer, Gloria G.
Elephants / by Gloria G. Schlaepfer
p. cm. — (Animalways)
Includes bibliographical references (p. 107) and index (p. 110).
ISBN 0-7614-1390-1
Elephants—Juvenile literature. [1. Elephants.] I. Title. II. Series.
QL737.P98 S34   2002   599.67—dc21   2001005592

Photo Research by Candlepants Incorporated

Cover Photo: Corbis / Papilio

The photographs in this book are used by permission and through the courtesy of:
Corbis, W. Perry Conway, title; Kevin Schafer, 9, 58; Jeremy Horner, 14; Hulton-Deutsch Collection, 18; Staffan Widstrand, 23; Jonathan Blair, 26; Gianni Dagli Orti, 28; Jim Richardson, 31; Reuters NewMedia Inc., 34, 89; Enzo & Paolo Ragazzini, 37; Annie Griffiths Belt, 39, 63; Ralph A. Clevenger, 41; M. Philip Kahl; Gallo Images, 43, 62, 68; Theo Allofs, 46, 72; Anthony Bannister; Gallo Images, 48, 79, 93 (left), 93 (right); Yann Arthur-Bertrand, 49, 65; Tony Wharton; Frank Lane Picture Agency, 50; Tom Brakefield, 51, 85; Gallo Images, 53, back cover; Eric and David Hosking, 56, 99; Lynda Richardson, 60; Galen Rowell, 61; Peter Johnson, 70; Ted Streshinsky, 75; Bettmann, 76; Dean Conger, 77; Mary Ann McDonald, 80; The Purcell Team, 84; Mary Ann McDonald, 87; Robert Gill; Papilio, 88; Tim Wright, 91; Charles O'Rear, 96; Karl Ammann, 97, 98; David Samuel Robbins, 101; *Art Resource, NY*: Giraudon, 16; Victoria & Albert Museum, London, 19, 20.

Printed in Italy
135642

Contents

Animal Kingdom

CNIDARIANS

coral

ARTHROPODS
(animals with jointed limbs and external skeleton)

MOLLUSKS

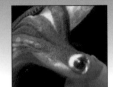

squid

CRUSTACEANS

crab

ARACHNIDS

spider

INSECTS

grasshopper

MYRIAPODS

centipede

CARNIVORES

lion

SEA MAMMALS

whale

PRIMATES

orangutan

HERBIVORES
(5 orders)

ELEPHANT

PHYLA

ANNELIDS

earthworm

CHORDATES
(animals with
a dorsal
nerve chord)

ECHINODERMS

starfish

**SUB
PHYLA**

VERTEBRATES
(animals with a
backbone)

CLASSES

FISH

fish

BIRDS

gull

MAMMALS

AMPHIBIANS

frog

REPTILES

snake

ORDERS

RODENTS

squirrel

INSECTIVORES

mole

MARSUPIALS

koala

SMALL MAMMALS
(several orders)

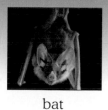

bat

1 The World of Elephants

> OF ALL WILD ANIMALS THE MOST EASILY TAMED AND
> THE GENTLEST IS THE ELEPHANT. IT COULD BE
> TAUGHT A NUMBER OF TRICKS, THE DRIFT AND
> MEANING OF WHICH IT UNDERSTANDS; . . . IT IS VERY
> SENSITIVE AND POSSESSED OF AN INTELLIGENCE
> SUPERIOR TO THAT OF OTHER ANIMALS.
>
> —Aristotle, writing between 345–342 B.C.

It is December, and the savanna is bone dry; the grass has been eaten down to stubs. The elephants know it is time to leave, and they head to the woodlands beyond the savanna. For the next few months, the small acacia trees will provide the elephants with food. They pick off leaves and twigs. They use their tusks to tear off bark before slowly chewing the wood to get its nutrients.

Three months later, when the long rains arrive, the elephants become restless. They are eager to leave the woodlands and return to the savanna with its sprouting green grasses. A large female elephant begins walking in the direction of the grassland.

ELEPHANTS PREFER GRASS TO ALL OTHER PLANT FOODS.

Her family—sisters, daughters, and their calves—follow. They join other families until a hundred or more elephants move together in one great herd. Bands of young males and solitary old bulls join the parade. The elephants walk with enthusiasm because they know that abundant food awaits them.

Megaherbivores

Elephants are the largest and most magnificent land animals. They are called *megaherbivores*. "Mega" means enormous and "herbivore" describes an animal that eats only plants. Everything about elephants is huge: gigantic bodies, a great appetite for food, enormous molars for grinding food, and massive incisor teeth called tusks.

Elephants are also the heaviest living land mammals, and they are surpassed in height only by giraffes. Two species from the large family of elephants exist today. The African elephant, *Loxodonta africana*, has large ears, a sloping forehead, and a lanky body. The rounder Asian, or Indian elephant, *Elephas maximus*, has a domed forehead and small ears. Although they are distinct species, the African elephant and the Asian elephant do share some physical characteristics and most behaviors.

The African Elephant, Loxodonta africana

Loxodonta africana, the African elephant, is the larger of the two species. *Loxodonta* means lozenge teeth, a description of the diamond-shaped ridges found on the animal's molars; *africana* refers to the continent where it lives.

Adult males, or bulls, are huge animals. They range from 7 to 12 feet (2.2 to 3.7 m) tall at the shoulder and can weigh up to 15,000 pounds (6,750 kg). Females, or cows, are about half the

African Elephant, Loxodonta africana

size of males. They may reach 9 feet (2.8 m) in height and weigh around 7,000 pounds (3,178 kg).

African elephants have dark gray or brown skin, a smooth forehead, and very large triangular ears that cover their shoulders.

Two subspecies, or types, of African elephants are recognized: *Loxodonta africana africana*, the savanna elephant, and *Loxodonta africana cyclotes*, the forest elephant. The forest elephant is smaller and darker than the savanna elephant, has smaller and more rounded ears, and thinner tusks that point downward.

At one time, biologists thought that the pygmy elephant was a third subspecies. Now it is generally believed that this small elephant that lives deep in the jungles and swamps of Central Africa is just a smaller version of *Loxodonta africana*.

The savanna elephant inhabits the grasslands, marshes, and woodlands of Africa's savanna lands. South of the Sahara Desert, savanna lands lie west to east in belts across Africa.

Savannas are subject to the extremes of climate—periods of heavy rainfall followed by months of drought. When the yearly rainfall averages 12 to 35 inches (30–89 cm), scattered thorny shrubs and trees appear on open grasslands. As rainfall increases to 35 to 60 inches (89–152 cm) a year, woody trees and shrubs take over.

The smaller forest elephant inhabits the warm tropical forests of West Africa and the Congo basin where it rains more than 60 inches (152 cm) in a year. The forests are rich in plants of all kinds—very tall evergreen trees, dense tangles of roots and plants growing on the ground, and climbing vines that snake from tree to tree. Forest elephants have a ready supply of food and water.

The Asian Elephant, Elephas maximus

Elephas maximus lives only in Southern and Southeastern Asia. Most Asian elephants are found in the forests, jungles, and grasslands of Myanmar, Thailand, Sri Lanka, Malaysia, India, Cambodia, Nepal, and Vietnam.

The elephants live in a variety of habitats from sea level to mountainous terrain. For example, in India, elephant habitat can be open grasslands, semi-tropical forests, or swampy plains. In those areas of Thailand that receive heavy rainfall, elephants live in lush tropical forests of palms, bamboo, and evergreen trees. In the valleys of Nepal, Asian elephants are found in grassy plains and woodlands.

The name *Elephas maximus* means the biggest elephant,

Asian Elephant, Elephas maximus

but it is actually smaller than the African elephant. An Asian bull can weigh as much as 9,400 pounds (4,268 kg) and stand 7.5 to 9 feet (2.4 to 2.9 m) tall. Cows are generally smaller, weighing about 6,600 pounds (3,000 kg) and measuring 8 feet (2.4 m) tall. The Asian elephant has two noticeable bulges above its forehead. The ears are half the size of African elephants and do not cover its shoulders.

Asian elephants have light gray skin that may become lighter with age. Albinos lack all pigment. Their skin is white, and they are very rare. In Southeast Asia, albinos are highly valued, and they have even been worshiped in Thailand. The albino elephant is also considered a bearer of good luck in India.

Four subspecies of *Elephas maximus* exist: *E. maximus max-*

THEIR SMALL
EARS, DOMED
FOREHEADS,
AND ARCHED
BACKS IDENTIFY
THESE BATHING
ASIAN
ELEPHANTS.

imus, the Ceylon elephant; *E. maximus hirsutus*, the Malaysian elephant; *E. maximus bengalensi*, the Indian elephant; and *E. maximus sumatranus*, the Sumatran elephant.

Elephants in Culture and History

Elephants are unique animals. Perhaps no other wild animal figures so prominently in the lives, myths, and popular culture of human society. People recognize that elephants are good-natured, faithful, intelligent creatures. And the elephant's great size and strength did not go unnoticed by people in the ancient world. At first, they hunted elephants for their meat and ivory. Around 4,000 to 5,000 years ago, the people in the Indus River Valley (modern day Pakistan) captured elephants, tamed them and trained them to be work animals in the forests. Their great strength enabled them to fell trees and carry the logs out of the forests. And then, slowly, elephants took on a new role—that of warriors. Exactly how it happened is not known. But as their mighty presence helped to win battles, more generals used them in their armies.

Elephants trained for warfare rather than work had to act against their generally peaceful nature. They learned to gore people with their tusks, trample on them, grab them with their trunks, throw them on the ground, and kill them. They were often the army's front line of offense. Soldiers who saw elephants for the first time were terrified and often ran away.

One of the earliest recorded battles that included elephants took place in 326 B.C. The Indian prince Porus had assembled a large army of soldiers, cavalry, chariots, and as many as 200 trained elephants. This massive force met the invading army of Alexander the Great in a bloody battle. Porus and his forces could not halt Alexander's mobile cavalry with its mounted archers, and Porus lost the fight.

Legend has it that Porus's elephant knelt next to the injured prince and gently took each spear out of his body with its trunk. The heroic prince survived, and Alexander, impressed by the prince's spirit, allowed him to remain ruler over his lands.

One of the best-known elephant campaigns is Hannibal's march through the Alps mountain range in France. At the time, Carthage, a city in North Africa, had been engaged in a series of battles with Rome over dominance of the Mediterranean region.

Hannibal, a Carthaginian general, decided to attack the Romans in their home country, Italy. In 218 B.C., Hannibal began his long campaign with an army of 30,000 soldiers and 37 elephants.

The army marched from Spain through southern France and managed the difficult crossing of the Rhone River by placing the elephants on rafts. Traveling through mountain passes in the Alps was very difficult for men and animals. The elephants proved to be good mountain climbers, however, and were a great help in removing rocks from the route to make the journey easier. They endured falling snow, icy conditions, mountain storms, and

A 16TH CENTURY PAINTING OF THE BATTLE OF ZAMA (202 B.C.), IN WHICH THE ROMAN COMMANDER SCIPIO AFRICANUS DEFEATED HANNIBAL'S ARMY.

hunger. In five months, Hannibal, his soldiers, and all thirty-seven elephants reached the Po Valley in Italy.

During their first fight with the Roman army, the elephants attacked fearlessly, and the Romans suffered significant losses. It was the elephant's last stand, though. In the months that followed, all thirty-seven died.

Elephants have continued to serve armies even in modern times, though no longer on the front lines. They have carried soldiers through dense jungles, helped build bridges, and moved supplies and equipment.

The Circus Elephant

Circuses go back thousands of years. The ancient Roman circus was a spectacle of chariot races and exotic wild animals. Elephants that were captured after battles became part of the circus. They quickly proved to be the favorites of the crowds. Animal trainers taught the elephants to kneel and bow before the emperor. They learned to walk on tightropes and to play simple musical instruments such as cymbals.

Other captive elephants were forced into cruel fights with starving lions or gladiators (warriors) armed with spears. While some Romans cheered at the bloody spectacle, others were overcome with compassion for the elephants. Nevertheless, elephants continued to be a highlight of the Roman circus.

Modern circuses began around 1800 in England, and elephants became one of the main attractions. They had only to walk into the circus tent to get loud applause. They performed headstands and walked upright on their hind legs.

Circus owners, such as Phineas Taylor Barnum, searched for something new and different to attract audiences. Barnum found it in the majestic Jumbo, an enormous African bull ele-

JUMBO POSES FOR A PICTURE WITH HIS KEEPER, MATTHEW SCOTT, AT THE ZOOLOGICAL GARDENS IN LONDON ABOUT 1882.

phant that lived in the London Zoo. In March 1882, Jumbo sailed to America and became a circus star in the Barnum & Bailey Circus. For the next three years, he delighted millions of adults and children. Then tragedy struck. Jumbo was hit and killed by a freight train. Newspapers carried the story on their front pages. People everywhere mourned his passing.

Elephants have continued to perform in traveling circuses over the last 200 years.

Elephants as Gods

Thousands of years ago, when people first tamed and trained elephants, they became partners in human activities. Elephants worked at felling trees and hauling logs out of the forest. They carried kings and princes on hunting trips and soldiers into battle.

The elephant became a symbol of power, greatness, and

rank among Indian royalty. They shared in princes' stature, glory, and richness, and were often dressed in ceremonial costumes. Elephants were also praised in song and legend, as this bit of Indian folklore explains: "An elephant mounted by a king is radiant; a king mounted on an elephant is resplendent; neither of the two outshines the other, elephants are consubstantial [united] with kings."

The elephant's image and qualities were blended into religious myths as well, and they still play an important part in Asian religions. One of the best examples is the Hindu god Ganesha, who has the head and trunk of an elephant and the body of a human. Protector of wisdom, learning, and prosperity, Ganesha is found in every temple in India. In addition, a stone elephant often guards temple entrances.

In Buddhism, elephant legends in the collection of stories called *Jakatas* help believers understand Buddha's life and messages. In one story, Buddha leaves a previous life to reappear as

INDRA, THE HINDU GOD OF WAR, IS SEATED ON A SPLENDIDLY ADORNED ELEPHANT CALLED AIRAVATA. THE PAINTING IS PROBABLY FROM THE OLD SOUTH INDIAN ARTISTIC CENTER TODAY CALLED TIRUCHCHIRAPPALLI, c. 1825.

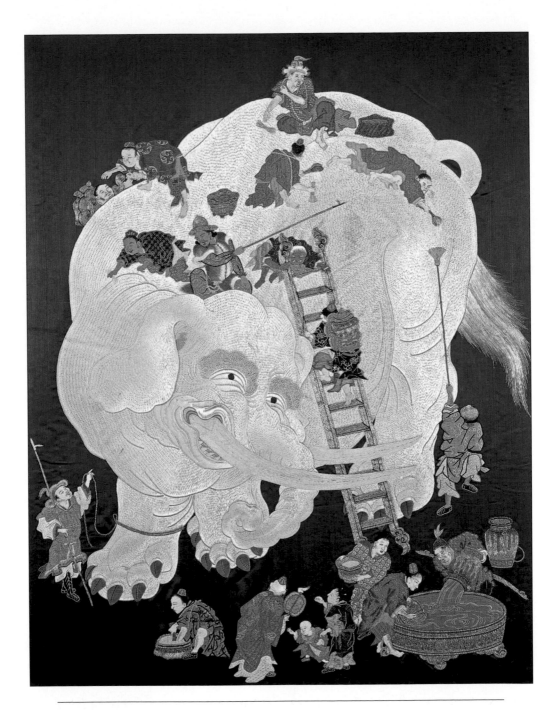

JAPANESE ART FROM THE 19TH CENTURY FEATURES A WHITE ELEPHANT BEING TENDED
TO BY ADMIRING HUMANS.

a snow-white elephant. He has six tusks and leads a herd of 8,000 flying elephants that have supernatural powers.

According to a legend about Buddha's birth, Queen Maya dreamt a supernatural being—a white elephant—came to her from heaven. The white elephant touched her side with a white lotus blossom. Nine months later, the queen gave birth to Siddhartha, the Buddha.

Popular Culture and Children's Stories

A favorite and familiar image, the elephant is found everywhere: in toys, jewelry, porcelain figurines, postage stamps, posters, television commercials, and art. Elephants are the heroes of countless stories, films, and cartoons. One example is the classic Disney movie *Dumbo*, a touching story of a brave baby elephant with big ears. The elephant is also the symbol of the United States's Republican Party.

Brave elephants in books and films delight children worldwide. Just about every American child knows the story, written by Jean de Brunhoff, of Babar, the little orphan elephant. Babar arrives in a city and makes friends with a nice old lady. He becomes a good student and well-behaved member of his human family. But he misses his earlier life, so he returns to the forest. There, the elephants recognize his wisdom and choose him to be their new king.

Elephant images have been part of human society for centuries. We respect and admire elephants for their loyalty, reliability, intelligence, and good nature. Given their long history of service to humans, it is easy to forget that elephants are a threatened wild species. They deserve our understanding of their natural ways and our continued protection.

2 Elephant Ancestors

The hunters push northward. Before them lie the huge tracks of a woolly mammoth, and the hunters run excitedly in the direction it is walking. Their clubs and stone-tipped spears are poised in readiness. They approach the animal silently, the wind blowing in their faces. The mammoth does not see or hear the humans as they creep closer and encircle it. When all is ready, the hunters pounce on the unsuspecting creature. Spears fly. They aim for the heart and head, and the mammoth rises up on its hind legs in anguish. It falls to its knees and collapses. The

THE BURIED FROZEN BODY OF THIS BABY MAMMOTH
WAS UNEARTHED IN 1977 IN SIBERIA.

primitive hunters work quickly to skin the mammoth and divide up the meat to carry back to camp.

Learning from Fossils

Within the first ten million years after the dinosaurs disappeared, another group of large animals began to evolve—the elephant's earliest ancestors. Those very early species had branched off from primitive ungulates, or hoofed mammals. During the next 60 million years, their descendants evolved into diverse and sometimes bizarre forms of elephantlike creatures. Our knowledge and understanding of them and their ways comes from scattered fossil remains.

A fossil record gives us clues about ancient life on Earth. The hard parts of animals, such as bones, teeth, and shells, or the woody parts of plants, are often preserved in rock, peat, tar, ice, or amber (the sticky resin from ancient trees). Sometimes footprints or even an impression of a body become fossilized. It is rare to find the preserved body of an extinct animal with its flesh, skin, and hair still intact, but it does happen.

In the spring of 1901, one of the most celebrated fossil discoveries occurred. A Lamut hunter (Siberian tribesman) stumbled upon a woolly mammoth, frozen and completely preserved in the ice. News sped west by telegraph across Siberia to the Imperial Academy of Sciences in Saint Petersburg, Russia. Russian zoologists were overjoyed; it was a rare opportunity to study this prehistoric giant.

A scientific expedition left Saint Petersburg at the end of May and traveled across southern Siberia by train to Irkutsk. From there, the group headed north and east by riverboat, horse, and reindeer-drawn cart. After a difficult four-month trip, the group reached the Beresovka River, near the Arctic Circle, the site of the find. A smell of decaying flesh filled the air. The mammoth's head and back—which stuck out of the permafrost layer, or permanently frozen ground—had been stripped clean of skin and flesh by wolves and other carnivores. The trunk and one of the tusks were also gone, but the rest of the body was intact.

The scientific team set up a makeshift cabin in which to thaw the rock-hard frozen soil, one layer at a time. The body was then separated from the soil and, to prevent the flesh from rotting, the partially thawed pieces were put outside to freeze again.

The scientists learned how the mammoth looked when it was alive. Its body was protected by a dense, woolly undercoat of fur. A bristly reddish-brown long outer coat covered that. The reddish-brown tail ended in a long, hairy tassel. Remarkably, pieces of grass clung to the mammoth's teeth, and 25 pounds (11.25 kg) of various plants were preserved in its stomach.

Thousands of years before its discovery, this woolly mammoth roamed the Arctic regions in search of food and fell into a hole in the ice. Unable to escape, it died there, its body locked and preserved in ice. The well-preserved Beresovka mammoth helped scientists learn more about the species' physical features, habits, and environment.

Proboscideans

Mammoths, elephants, and their distant relatives, such as paleo-mastodons, belong to a large order of animals called Proboscidea, meaning animals with a long trunk or proboscis. Throughout their history, more than 150 proboscideans evolved, inhabited many different habitats and continents, and eventually died out.

Proboscideans are recognized by their massive bodies, flexible trunks, and pillarlike legs. As the proboscideans evolved, their six cheek teeth, in each half of their jaws, were replaced by giant

THE RECONSTRUCTION OF AN ADULT MAMMOTH, *MAMMUTHUS PRIMIGENIUS*, SHOWS THE LONG CURVING TUSKS, SMALL EARS, AND LONG, WOOLLY COAT OF THE EXTINCT SPECIES.

chewing teeth. Their second incisor teeth gradually developed into great tusks. Some species had tusks in the upper jaw, others in the lower jaw, and a few had tusks in both jaws. The necks of later proboscideans became shorter as they evolved larger and heavier bodies. The skull continued to enlarge to support the trunk and heavy teeth.

One of the very first animals recognized as a distant relative of elephants was *Moeritherium*. It lived in the swampy regions of Africa from 35 to 50 million years ago. Its fossilized bones were first discovered in 1901 at the El Faiyum oasis, near the Nile River in Egypt.

Moeritherium was about the size of a pig and was probably a stocky animal with sturdy elephantlike legs. Although it may not have looked like an elephant, its snout, or nose, was somewhat elongated. It resembled a modern tapir, a hoofed mammal that lives in the forests of Asia and South America. The thick second incisor teeth on each side of its jaw are thought to be the forerunners of tusks.

Throughout the Tertiary Period, which extended from about 10 to 65 million years ago, many species of early proboscideans evolved and lived together. Each adapted to a specific ecological niche, or place in the environment.

Many of the new species spread out from their African origins to other continents. The paleomastodons gave rise to the gomphotheres, the Mammutidae, the stegodonts, and the Elephantidae. A separate family, the Deinotheridae, evolved with the others.

The Deinotheres and Gomphotheres

The giant deinotheres emerged in Africa about 25 million years ago, at the same time as mastodons, other elephantlike mammals. Although they looked like modern elephants, their molars, or grinding teeth, were so different that scientists place them in a family of their own. The deinotheres had no tusks in their upper jaws. Rather, their tusks extended from the lower jaws and curved downward, enabling them to dig out plants and roots. The giant deinotheres lived for about 24 million years, dispersing to Europe and Southeast Asia.

Phiomia was another early proboscidean that lived in Africa 25 to 40 million years ago. It had two downward-curving tusks in its upper jaw and two straight tusks in its lower jaw. Its skull was elongated so it had an elephantlike appearance.

IN THIS RECONSTRUCTION, AN ARTIST HAS DEPICTED STONE AGE HUNTERS BRINGING DOWN A MAMMOTH USING ONLY THEIR WOODEN SPEARS.

Descendants of *Phiomia* were the gomphotheres, the most widespread of the proboscideans. Skeletons of this group have been found throughout Africa, Eurasia, and the Americas.

One of them, *Gomphotherium angustidens*, lived about 20 million years ago and stood about 10 feet (3 m) in height. Its cheek, or chewing, teeth had low blunt crowns, and they were covered with thick enamel and capped with cementum, a bonelike protective material. *Gomphotherium* had two sets of tusks: two long upper tusks and two short broad tusks in its elongated lower jaw. The lower tusks, which acted like shovels, gave the animals their names—*Gompotherium* means shovel tuskers.

From the gomphotheres, two main branches evolved, the Elephantidae family, and the Mammutidae and Stegodontidae families, which are now extinct.

The Sturdy Mastodons

Mastodons are often confused with mammoths. Some of the confusion may come from their scientific names. Mastodons belong to the family Mammutidae, and the mammoth's genus name is *Mammuthus*. In addition, both of these extinct elephants lived at the same time, shared some physical characteristics, and occupied similar habitats.

Mastodons descended from the paleomastodons around 25 million years ago. Mastodons spread widely throughout the world, reaching North America about 7 million years ago. They moved to South America a few million years later when sea levels dropped during the Pleistocene ice ages.

Mastodons were shorter than both mammoths and modern elephants. Sturdily built, their bodies were covered with long reddish-brown hair. One species, *Mammut americanum*, the American mastodon, adapted to cold climates and survived until ten thousand years ago. In comparison to living elephants, the mastodon's small, low-crowned grinding teeth are described as primitive. Mastodons fed mainly on leaves, avoiding woody plants, which they were unable to chew.

The Stegodontidae Family

The stegodonts evolved at the same geological time as mastodons. They resembled mastodons in body form and head shape but the structure of their teeth differed. The Stegodontidae family is made up of the *Stegolophodon* and *Stegodon* genus. *Stegolophodon* is considered an intermediate genus between the mastodons and present-day elephants. It first appeared about 40 million years ago and lived in Africa, Europe, and Asia until the Pleistocene epoch. *Stegodon*, which evolved from *Stegolophodon*, appeared in Asia 14 million years ago. As sea levels dropped during the Pleistocene ice ages some 10,000 to 650,000 years ago, some stegodonts used land bridges to seek new foraging areas in the Philippines and on Indonesian islands. Many thousands of years later the climate warmed again, the ice slowly melted, and sea levels rose again. The *Stegodonts* were stranded on the islands. Over time, they grew smaller and smaller until pygmy forms developed, standing less that 3 feet (1 m) tall.

In contrast, the stegodonts on the continents continued to have large bodies and long tusks. *Stegodon ganesa* had long parallel tusks that grew so close together that there was little room for the animal's trunk. Because this species was found in India until about one million years ago, it was named after the Hindu god Ganesha.

From the large group of giant proboscideans, the ancestors of mammoths and modern elephants evolved around 16 million years ago. An early example is *Primelephas*. It still had small lower tusks, but its upper tusks grew long and strong. An important change occurred in the grinding surfaces of its molars. They formed low-crowned intersecting ridges of dentin, the material that teeth are made of, and they were covered by hard enamel. The areas between the ridges contained a large amount of cementum. These large, widespreading chewing teeth were

A PALEONTOLOGIST HOLDS A FOSSIL IN HIS DIGS AT HOT SPRINGS, SOUTH DAKOTA.

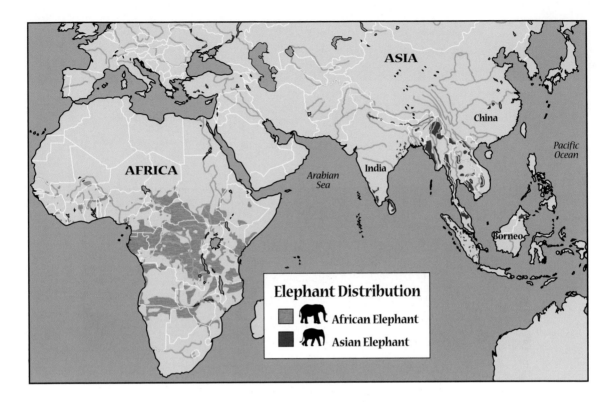

Elephant Distribution
- African Elephant
- Asian Elephant

clearly an intermediary step in elephant evolution, that allowed *Primelephas* to eat a variety of plants.

The Elephantidae Family

From *Primelephas*, the family Elephantidae emerged. It includes mammoths, African elephants, and Asian elephants. With Elephantidae, the trend toward large molars reached its peak. The molars occur in cycles, with only one at a time in each side of the jaw. The number of lamellae, or plates, increases so there is more tooth available for cutting and chewing. To offset the weight of the large tooth, the enamel is thinner. Finally, the crowns, or tops, of the molars are very high, so the teeth wear away slowly. Elephants, like mammoths did, eat grasses, leaves, and the woody parts of shrubs and trees.

The woolly mammoth is one of seven known mammoth species. Mammoth means immense or gigantic—all mammoths were huge creatures with large, long, curving tusks. Their ancestor evolved in Africa three million years ago, and mammoths slowly spread to Europe and Asia. During the Ice Ages, the seas were locked in ice, and the Bering Strait, between Asia and North America, became a corridor for travel. Mammoths, humans, and other animals used a land bridge there to reach North America.

The best known of all the mammoth species is the woolly mammoth, *Mammuthus primigenius*. Fossil remains and preserved bodies have enabled us to learn about this species. It was one of the largest members of the family Elephantidae, standing 10.8 feet (3.3 m) tall, a height similar to the Asian elephant. The mammoth's body, however, was shorter, and the lower portion of its back sloped downward. Its high, dome-shaped skull was covered by a reserve of fat, as were its shoulders. A 3-inch-thick (7.5 cm-thick) layer of fat under its tough skin protected its entire body from the severe weather of the frozen northlands. The mammoth's tusks were enormous, long, and curved into a circle. Males had particularly long tusks, with some as long as 15.7 feet (4.8 m). The tusks probably acted like shovels, scraping away snow from buried grasses and low-growing shrubs.

The woolly mammoth survived most of the one-and-a-half-million-year-long ice ages of the Pleistocene epoch. But when the last ice age ended about 10,000 years ago, most mammoths died out, along with the mastodons. Some scientists place the blame for their extinction on Stone Age hunters. Other scientists believe a combination of factors led to their extinction. For instance, recent studies point to an abrupt change in climate during that time period. A warming period following the cold of the ice ages would have directly affected the plants available to

the mammoths. They may not have been able to adapt to new
vegetation. Unable to adapt or get enough to eat, their population would have diminished. Disease may also have played a
role in their decline.

If this were so, it would have become possible for early
hunters to overcome a mammoth weakened and stressed by ill-
ness or starvation using only clubs or stone-tipped spears.
However it happened, the extinction of mammoths and mastodons meant that only the Asian elephant and the African elephant
species remain today.

CLASSIFICATION

Scientists classify all living organisms into smaller and smaller groups that have more and more features in common. The classification of the two living elephant species is shown below.

Kingdom: Animalia (animals)

Phylum: Chordata (animals with spinal columns)

Class: Mammalia (warm-blooded animals)

Order: Proboscidie (animals with trunks)

Suborder: Elephantoidea (animals with elephantlike forms)

Family: Elephantidae (elephants)

African elephant genus: Loxodonta

African elephant species: africana

Asian elephant genus: Elephas

Asian elephant species: maximus

Asian and African Elephants

Three million years ago, as the mammoths evolved in Africa, another evolutionary line appeared in Africa that led to *Elephas*, the Asian elephant. *Elephas* effectively spread out of Africa to southern Europe and Asia. One successful species, *Elephas antiquus*, the forest elephant, inhabited the thickly forested regions of southern Europe and Asia between 70,000 to 500,000 years ago. That species died out as the ice moved south at the start of the Würm Glacial Age, 75,000 years ago.

One and a half million years ago, the newest elephant species, *Loxodonta africana*, the African elephant, appeared. Unlike the other species, *Loxodonta* did not leave Africa. Throughout the Pleistocene epoch, it ranged throughout the entire continent, even across the Sahara Desert. The region, at that time, had sufficient vegetation to support elephants.

3 The Remarkable Nature of Elephants

COVERED IN A ROUGH LOOSE-SKINNED ARMOR THE COLOR
OF STONES, RICH IN IVORY, BOADICEA'S POLISHED TUSKS
STOOD OUT LIKE WEAPONS, AND I COULD IMAGINE THIS
GREAT PACHYDERM PREPARING FOR BATTLE.

From *Among the Elephants* by Iain Douglas-Hamilton, 1975

Asked to name an animal that is as big as a truck, with a nose that reaches its toes, everyone would get it right: elephant. An elephant's remarkable trunk is an organ almost without limits. It can bend, twist, stretch, and curl. An elephant uses its trunk as we do our arms, hands, and fingers. When you cry, you wipe the tears away with your hand. An elephant wipes secretions from its eyes with its trunk. Just as we use our arms to caress and hug, a grown elephant wraps its trunk around a young calf to comfort and protect it.

A WORKING ELEPHANT SLIDES ITS TUSKS UNDER A
LOG AND USES ITS TRUNK TO HOLD AND MOVE IT.

The trunk can also be very powerful. An elephant can use its trunk to lift and carry objects as large as a 600-pound (270 kg) log. The trunk is so strong that it can tear branches off a tree, yet it can delicately pick up something as small as a peanut.

The trunk begins at the upper jaw. It is a continuation of the nose and upper lip in one long, boneless appendage. Two tubular nostrils run through the center of the trunk, surrounded by bundles of muscles, nerve cells, and blood vessels. The trunk ends in a fleshy, triangular, fingerlike projection. African elephants' trunks have two "fingers" opposite one another. They use them as we do our thumb and index finger, to grasp small objects. Asian elephants' trunks have only one finger. These elephants are more apt to tightly curl the end of their trunks around small items to pick them up.

The trunk's most important function is to get food and water into the mouth. As it feeds on long grasses, an elephant uses its trunk like a hand to curl and twist around the grass blades. Then, grasping tightly, the elephant uses its trunk to pull out the clump, shake the dirt off the roots, and stuff everything into its mouth.

If leaves or fruits on a tall tree are out of reach, elephants stretch out their trunks to grab them. Occasionally, they will balance on their hind legs to reach up even farther than a giraffe.

It probably would not occur to you to drink through your nose, but that's what an elephant does. It sucks up water into its nostrils and seals the end with its fingers so the water doesn't run out. Then it puts the tip of the trunk into its mouth, tilts up its head, and lets the water run down into its throat. An adult elephant can pull up a gallon or two (4 to 8 l) of water at one time and drink as much as 25 to 60 gallons (95 to 227 l) a day. In hot weather, elephants take cooling showers by filling up their trunks with water and spraying their bodies.

THE TRUNK OF AN AFRICAN ELEPHANT HAS BUMPS ALONG ITS EDGES AND IS QUITE WRINKLY. THE TIP HAS TWO OPPOSING TRIANGULAR "FINGERS."

No other animal has a limb or body part as versatile as the elephant's trunk. In addition to all the other abilities of the trunk, it is the vehicle for the animal's keen senses of smell and touch. In fact, scientists say that no animal has a better nose. Elephants wave their trunks in the air to learn about their environment. They can smell water that is miles away. A male will place his trunk on a female's body and sniff to find out if she is ready to mate.

The sensitive trunk can tell whether something is rough or smooth, hot or cold. The trunk even gives elephants a sure footing on a difficult or unfamiliar surface. The trunk feels the way, and the feet follow.

Tusks, Useful Tools

As remarkable as the trunk is, an elephant's ivory tusks give the large animal its distinctive appearance. Tusks are simply long, hollow incisor teeth made of a hard material called dentin. The tusks are covered with a hard, creamy-white enamel, resulting in ivory. Two-thirds of each tusk is visible, while the rest is hidden within the skull. Despite their awesome appearance, tusks are used more as tools than as weapons. Tusks are the pickaxes an elephant uses to scrape and dig in soil and rocks to find water and salt. The tusks become crowbars when the animal tears away strips of bark from a tree or harvests fleshy roots for food.

Both female and male African elephants develop tusks. A female's tusks grow slowly but continuously. They don't get as heavy as males' tusks and are generally more slender. The tusks of males keep growing longer and heavier throughout their lives. For example, a tusk of a 10-year-old bull elephant may weigh about 11 pounds (5 kg); at 30 years of age, the tusk's weight increases to 45 pounds (20.5 kg). When the big male dies of old age at 60, its tusks will be twice as heavy, from 110 to 175

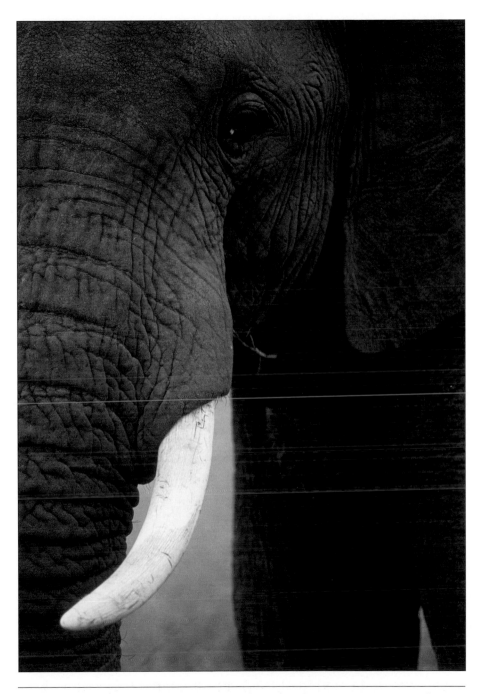

AN ELEPHANT'S TUSKS ARE MODIFIED INCISOR TEETH. ONE-THIRD OF THE TUSK'S LENGTH IS HIDDEN WITHIN THE UPPER JAW.

pounds (49.9-79.45 kg). The average tusk length for both males and females is 5.9 feet (1.8 m).

The largest tusks on record came from a huge bull killed in Kenya in 1899. It was reported that one of its tusks weighed 224 pounds (102 kg) and the other 211 pounds (96 kg). Tusks of that size are not seen today. In the last century, poachers and hunters sought out and killed the elephants with the biggest tusks because ivory is so valuable.

Among Asian elephants, only bulls develop tusks. Female Asian elephants have incisor teeth that are short and rarely protrude far enough from the jaw to be seen. Males' tusks average 4.9 feet (1.5 m) in length and weigh about 35 pounds (16 kg). However, some Asian bulls are tuskless.

Elephants tend to favor one tusk over another, just as humans are right-handed or left-handed. As a result, one tusk usually wears down more than the other.

Teeth, Big as Bricks

Throughout the long evolutionary history of proboscideans, the grinding teeth, or molars, slowly changed to accommodate an extensive and varied diet of plant foods. An elephant's molars are high-crowned and huge—about one foot (30 cm) long and weighing 4 pounds (1.8 kg). There are four molars, two on each side of the jaw, one above and one below. The combination of muscular jaws and four large molars enables the elephant to grind up the toughest plant material.

Unlike other mammals whose new teeth erupt and push up from underneath, an elephant's new molars develop at the back of the jaw. As the old molars wear down and begin to break off in pieces, a new set of slightly bigger teeth slowly moves forward to replace them. In that way, an elephant goes through six sets of

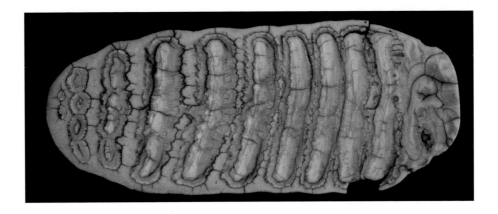

A FOSSILIZED ELEPHANT TOOTH IS DISPLAYED.

molars during its lifetime. Each set consists of the four grinding teeth. The last set advances into position when the animal is about forty years old. Like a human's adult teeth, these must last the elephant for the rest of its life. As the animal approaches old age, it may no longer be able to chew well. Unfortunately, that can lead to malnutrition and starvation.

An elephant's molars are actually plates joined together into a single oblong tooth. Elephants chew by moving their lower jaw backward and forward. As the teeth wear down, a series of complex ridges, or grooves, are exposed. The ridges extend from side to side, unlike those of most other herbivores. In cattle, for instance, the ridges run the length of the molars, and the cattle chew from side to side.

The pattern of the ridges is an important part of the scientific classification of elephants. The ridges on an African elephant's molars are diamond-shaped, while the ridges are parallel to one another in the Asian elephant. As the elephant grows, its molars increase in size, the ridges increase in number, and chewing becomes more effective. At birth, an African elephant's molars have three ridges. The molars in the sixth and last set have ten ridges. An Asian elephant's first molars have four ridges. In the last set, at age forty to forty-five, there are as many as twenty-four.

The surfaces of the teeth are covered with protective hard dental enamel, and the spaces in between with softer dental cement. The teeth therefore wear down very slowly. An elephant gets its fifth set of molars at age twenty-five, and those teeth will chew, chomp, crack, and grind food for twenty years, until the last set pushes forward.

Lightweight Skull

An elephant's massive skull helps support its heavy trunk, tusks, and teeth. Yet the bones in the skull are not solid. Instead, the skull contains a maze of extensive cavities, or hollow spaces. They provide stability and at the same time reduce the skull's weight. Solid bone would make the head too heavy for the elephant to carry it easily.

Asian elephants differ from African elephants in the shape of their skulls. The tops of Asian elephants' heads have two noticeable domes, side by side. The foreheads of African elephants form a smooth curve.

Inside the skull lies the brain, the largest and heaviest of any land mammal. It weighs about 12 pounds (5.5 kg). A human brain weighs about 3 pounds (1.4 kg).

Supporting Bones

One can only marvel at an elephant's massive size and the skeleton that supports all that weight. A long spine and thick ribs support the muscles and internal organs. The large leg bones are placed one above the other to form strong pillars. In this way, an elephant can relax and not topple over.

Elephant Skeleton

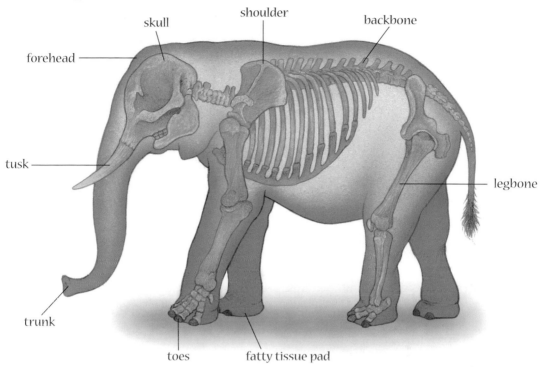

forehead

skull

shoulder

backbone

tusk

legbone

trunk

toes

fatty tissue pad

The elephant's feet are also constructed to bear up under its great weight. Amazingly, an elephant walks on its toes. Its weight is supported by the tip of each toe and the thick cushion that serves as the heel. The foot is nearly round and rests on a spongy layer of skin that cushions and absorbs the impact of the foot on the ground as the elephant walks.

When an elephant stands, its weight causes each foot to expand. As the foot is lifted with each step, it contracts, or becomes smaller. The thick soles of the feet are cracked and grooved rather than smooth, and the soles grip the ground, as athletic shoes do, so elephants can easily climb steep hills and walk on rocks and other rough surfaces.

Elephants step briskly and almost soundlessly, averaging 3.7

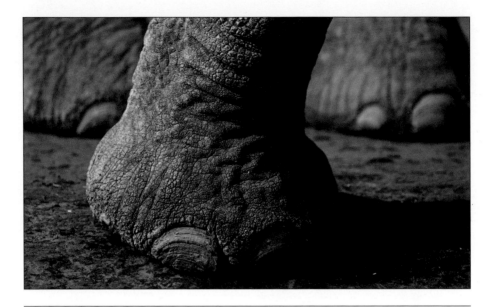

WHEN RESTING ON THE GROUND, AN ELEPHANT'S FOOT IS FLAT-SOLED AND ROUND. THERE ARE USUALLY FOUR OR FIVE TOENAILS ON EACH FOREFOOT IN BOTH AFRICAN AND ASIAN ELEPHANTS, BUT ONLY THREE BACK TOES ON AN AFRICAN ELEPHANT. ASIAN ELEPHANTS HAVE FOUR OR FIVE BACK TOES.

to 5 miles (6–8 km) per hour. If they are in a hurry to get somewhere, such as a watering hole, they'll take long, fast strides. They can even run at speeds of up to 30 miles (48 km) per hour for short distances.

A Big Animal with a Big Appetite

Elephants have internal organs similar to other mammals. But as you might expect, everything about an elephant is bigger. An adult elephant's heart is not only five times larger than a human's; it is also fifty times as heavy!

Eating is the number one activity for elephants. They spend about sixteen hours a day foraging and feeding. They can eat most plant parts. Tough grasses, leaves, fruits, twigs, and bark from shrubs and trees are all part of their diet. In the wild, an adult consumes between 220 and 400 pounds (100 and 200 kg) of plant matter and drinks 18 to 40 gallons (68 to 151 l) of water daily. The intestines of adult elephants are longer than any other mammal's, yet elephants digest and absorb only about 40 percent of the food they swallow.

Unlike cud-chewing animals, or ruminants, such as sheep and cows, elephants cannot digest cellulose very well. Cellulose is the tough material that makes up the walls of plant cells. The bacteria needed to break down cellulose are in short supply in an elephant's gut.

To aid digestion, however, elephants have a very large

Elephant Organs

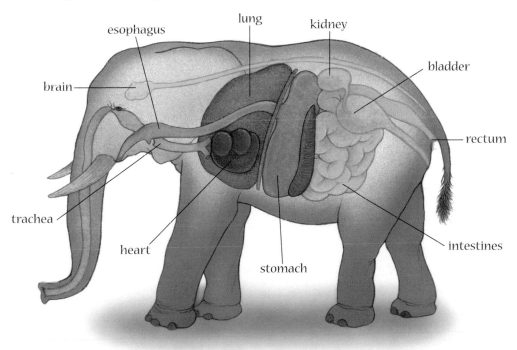

cecum, or extra chamber, located at the junction of the small and large intestines. The cecum is populated with bacteria and protozoa (single-celled organisms). These organisms digest the proteins, sugars, and starches found in bulky plant foods.

Digestion may take up to forty-six hours—almost two days! The partially digested plant fibers and seeds as well as intact seeds are excreted as dung or manure. Dung provides a bonanza of benefits to the plant and animal community. Dung improves soil texture and, because it is a natural fertilizer, enriches the soil for plant growth. Seeds that escaped digestion are carried in the dung to new areas to germinate. Monkeys, baboons, and duiker antelopes routinely pick through dung to search for edible seeds. Scarabs, or dung beetles, lay their eggs in dung pellets, giving their offspring a ready source of food upon hatching.

DUNG BEETLES LAY THEIR EGGS IN ELEPHANT DUNG, AND THEIR YOUNG FEED ON IT AFTER THEY HATCH.

Wrinkly Skin and Keeping Cool

Humans are born with smooth, soft skin that becomes wrinkled in old age. Elephant skin starts out somewhat wrinkled at birth. Wrinkles increase as the animal ages, and the skin takes on a

THE CRACKS AND GROOVES IN AN ELEPHANT'S SKIN PROVIDE MORE SURFACE AREA TO TRAP WATER AND MUD, WHICH PROTECTS THE SKIN FROM SUNBURN AND HELPS TO COOL THE BODY.

leathery appearance. Elephant skin is also thick. In fact, elephants are also called pachyderms, a Greek word meaning thick-skinned. The skin of an adult elephant is thickest on its back, up to 1 inch (3 cm) thick. In comparison, human skin measures no more than 1/16 to 1/8 inch (1.6 to 3 mm) thick.

Despite its thickness, elephants' skin is quite sensitive. Elephants are plagued by biting flies, blood-sucking ticks, leeches, and biting mosquitoes. The giants often roll in the mud or throw sand and dirt over their bodies to help protect against the bites of these pests. They rub against rocks and tree trunks to knock off ticks.

Rolling in mud also helps elephants stay cool. Biologists are not sure if elephants have sweat glands in their skin. For many mammals, including humans, sweat glands help the body remove heat. As sweat on the skin evaporates, the body cools down. But elephants have other ways to keep cool.

For example, elephants love to soak in watering holes, spray water over themselves, or roll in mud. The grooves and cracks of their wrinkly skin increase its surface area and trap moisture, so evaporation takes longer. The elephant's wrinkly skin is better at cooling than smooth skin would be. Elephants also rest in the shade during the hotter midday hours.

And, most importantly, their ears operate like natural fans. Asian elephants have small triangular earflaps. African elephants have the biggest ears in the world. The ears of a big bull can be 6.5 feet by 5 feet (2 m by 1.5 m). (Some people think they are shaped like the continent of Africa.) Their large surface area is laced with blood vessels that allow body heat to escape into the air. As elephants flap their ears, the blood in their veins cools

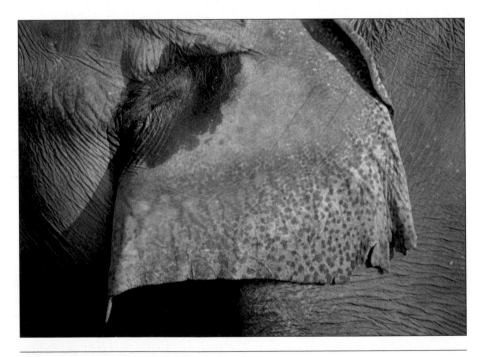

THE VERY LARGE EARS OF AFRICAN ELEPHANTS ACT LIKE FANS WHEN FLAPPED AND HELP KEEP THE ANIMALS COOL.

ELEPHANT CALVES REGULARLY PLAY IN WATER LIKE CHILDREN.

down. Then the cooled blood circulates back through the body. Flapping its ears fans the elephant's body with moving air, just like an electric fan would. If it is windy, elephants simply turn their backs to the wind and hold their ears out to cool down.

4 Elephant Behavior

Well before dawn, the matriarch stirs from her night's sleep. Her family, sensing her movements, wakes up and gathers around her. Slowly, they set out on a familiar path to the feeding grounds, picking up and eating tidbits along the way. The oldest female sets the pace and leads the group.

Elephants are highly social animals. On the African savannas, female elephants live in small stable family groups of nine or more, headed by the oldest female, the matriarch. Within the family are several generations of sisters and daughters and their young calves, both male and female. A family of forest elephants, on the other hand, may consist of only a single female and her male and female calves.

WITH ITS LONG STRETCHY TRUNK, THIS ELEPHANT IS ABLE TO REACH THE HIGHEST LEAVES ON THE TREE.

The matriarch is responsible for her family's safety, food, and water. She knows the paths that lead to feeding areas in all seasons, where to find trees with ripe fruit, where to find water in times of drought. She gained her vast knowledge from watching her mother, who learned from her mother. As the uncontested leader, the matriarch decides where they will graze, bathe, and sleep.

Family members stay near her. They are always alert to the matriarch's presence, where she is and what she is doing. When she moves, they close in behind her and follow. If there is a question of danger, they look to her and follow her example. If she calls them with a low rumble, they head straight to her. She holds the family together in good times and bad—their leader, without question.

The Daily Schedule

Most of what is known about elephant life comes from studies of the African savanna elephant. Asian and African forest elephants are sheltered within rain forests, making it more difficult to observe them. Nevertheless, all elephants require plenty of food, fresh water, and shade.

African savanna elephants have a fairly regular routine that is centered on the need to eat frequently. They feed until midday, then they rest in the shade during the hottest hours. Bathing, socializing, and more feeding may follow throughout the evening. Before midnight, they head to a secure place to sleep.

Elephants are awesome eating machines. They graze in one place until the food is gone; then they often travel several miles to find new vegetation. In areas with high amounts of rainfall and lots of plant foods, elephants may be able to stay within an area as small as 100 square miles (250 km^2).

On the other hand, elephants living in semi-desert regions, such as Namibia, Africa, are on an endless journey for food and water. Their best sources of water might be 40 miles (64 km) from their feeding grounds.

In the African savanna, the seasons determine where food will be found. Elephants are migratory herbivores, as are zebras, wildebeests, cape buffaloes, and many antelopes. The animals time their movements to the rainy season and the return of nutritious green grasses. The long rains usually arrive in East Africa in mid-March and continue through May. A long dry season follows until November and December, when the short rains appear.

Asian elephants, like their African cousins, browse, or eat, green leaves, fruit, delectable new plant shoots, and the soft bark of young trees. They also graze in the grasslands surrounding forests.

As herbivores, elephants eat many kinds of plants and plant parts. Knowledge is passed down from mother to calf so the animals recognize which plants are tasty and not poisonous. When foraging is good, grass makes up the bulk of their diet. Even forest elephants search out grassy meadows to dine in. Grass is not only nutritious, but it has a higher water content than foliage, and it is easy to gather up and eat. Among elephants, there is little or no competition for food. However, the oldest animals in the family group graze on the best grasses.

As the ground dries up and the grass becomes less appealing, elephants pull leaves and berries off shrubs, snap twigs, and strip bark from trees. Woody food is not as easily digested as grass, but it fills the elephant's enormous stomach. Unlike grass, which the elephant chews briefly, woody food requires more preparation—the teeth must grind twigs, foliage, and bark more thoroughly before they can be swallowed.

ELEPHANTS PRY OFF BARK WITH THEIR TUSKS. BARK PROVIDES MINERALS IN THEIR DIET, BUT REMOVING ALL THE BARK FROM A TREE CAN DESTROY IT.

If a dry period in the savanna extends into a drought and food is very scarce, savanna elephants can become quite destructive in their search for food. They strip shrubs bare of leaves. The elephants knock down or uproot trees to get to the leaves at the very top. Any plants left in an area are eaten. If the drought is prolonged, many animals starve.

Impact of Elephants

Elephants are a key species throughout the savannas and forests where they live. The landscape is changed by their numbers, eating patterns, and seasonal migrations. By browsing leaves, twigs, and branches from shrubs and trees, they create openings in dense woodlands and keep woody plants from spreading into the grasslands. Elephant eating patterns allow sunlight to reach the ground in thick forests so that plants will grow. Throughout their long history, elephant herds have shaped the ecology of their environment.

Lovers of Water

Elephants require water and they can never be far from it. During the dry season, they stay near permanent water holes—ones that almost never dry up. Sometimes, though, water is not visible at the surface. But elephants know where to find water and how to get at it. First they loosen the soil with their tusks. Then they use their trunks to dig until the water percolates up from the ground. Often, elephants will get down on all four knees to widen and deepen the hole. During a drought, these watering holes are lifesavers for the other animals who share the elephants' environment. When the rains start again, elephants return to their familiar feeding grounds to enjoy the new supply of green grass and watering holes and rivers swollen with rainwater.

Generally, elephants quench their thirst once a day if water is close by. Sometimes, though, they must travel miles between their feeding area and a water source. When that happens, they can go for about three days without water.

After satisfying their thirst, they linger in the water to enjoy a bath or rejoice in a roll in the mud. If the water is deep enough, they may submerge their bodies completely, using their trunks as snorkels to breathe through. They spray water over themselves and others. They splash, churn up the mud, and roll around in it until the protective ooze covers their skin.

The time spent at the watering hole nourishes the spirit as well as the body. For calves and adolescents, it is a chance to play with siblings and cousins. They climb over one another, wiggling, squealing, and splashing with their trunks—just as children do when they are having a good time.

As big as they are, elephants are surprisingly good swimmers and can swim several miles at a time. They have been observed swimming across wide rivers to reach islands. They even swim in the ocean. When elephants swim, they hold their trunks upright so they can breathe. In a river with a fast current, mothers

ON ITS KNEES, THIS AFRICAN ELEPHANT DIGS DEEPER FOR WATER HIDDEN UNDER THE GROUND.

keep their calves from being swept away by swimming beside them, blocking the current with their own bodies.

Salt Mining

Animals that are strict herbivores, such as elephants, often crave salt and other minerals that are largely missing from their regular diet.

Zebras and buffaloes lick salt-laden rocks or soil. Elephants do not lick because their tongues are not long enough. Instead, they dig up the earth with their tusks. Then they take chunks of soil or rock into their mouths. They grind up the chunks into a powder with their large molars before swallowing it.

Elephants will even risk danger in search of salt crystals. For example, forest elephants living near Mount Elgon, an extinct volcano in Kenya, go into the totally dark deep underground Kitum Cave, seeking salt. The families walk single file into the cave, head to tail. They feel their way along the dangerous paths with their sensitive trunks. The mineral-rich volcanic rock is so hard that the elephants must use their tusks to chip out bits of it. Years of mining in that way have reduced their tusks to mere stumps. Scientists who analyzed the rock found it contains minerals that promote good health.

Enemies

Given their great size and strength, adult elephants have no natural enemies. On rare occasions, though, lions in Africa or tigers in Asia are so desperately hungry that they try to capture and kill a baby elephant. The elephant herd responds by encircling all the infants. The adults face outward and confront the enemy. Even a lion or tiger is no match for an adult elephant. If threats

ELEPHANTS WATCH A NEARBY MALE LION TO BE SURE THEIR CALVES ARE SAFE.

do not scare the predator away, an elephant will charge the attacking carnivore and crush it to death.

The greatest threat to elephants, though, comes from humans. A herd is defenseless against guns and semi-automatic weapons, which can slaughter the animals within a few minutes.

Deadly Diseases

Wild elephants are generally healthy, but they can become ill from a number of diseases, some of which are fatal. One of the deadliest is anthrax, a naturally occurring disease that affects many animals with fever, chills, diarrhea, and convulsions. Often entire families of elephants are killed by anthrax.

Only elephants experience paralysis of the trunk and elephant pox. With pox, blisterlike swellings appear in the mouth, on the trunk, legs, and between the toes. Elephants in captivity who receive prompt medical treatment can be saved. Without treatment, the elephant may die.

Elephants get sick from some of the same illnesses we do: colds, intestinal disorders, rashes, tuberculosis, and pneumonia. In their natural environment, elephants have ways of healing themselves. If they have a stomachache, they may fast or eat bitter-tasting herbs and bark. If wounded, they smear mud on the sore to cover it and keep it from getting infected.

A MAHOUT (ANIMAL TRAINER) TAKES HIS ELEPHANT OUT TO THE RIVER FOR ITS DAILY BATH.

TWO YOUNG AFRICAN ELEPHANTS ENTWINE TRUNKS AND CLASH TUSKS IN A TEST OF THEIR STRENGTH.

Death

Typically, elephants live fifty-five to sixty-five years. They show their age just as other animals do. Their bodies get thinner and their skin gets more wrinkled. Their faces and heads become gaunt and their eyes look sunken. An old elephant grows weak, walks more slowly, and is unable to keep up with its family. It eventually falls back to die. But an elephant family will never knowingly abandon one of its members.

Biologists have observed elephants going to the aid of a dying family member. They try to support it and coax it to get up. They gently touch the dying animal with their trunks and stand with it silently as it dies. They may even cover the dead elephant's body with branches and dirt.

Within days, the body all but disappears as scavengers—

vultures, jackals, and hyenas—eat the meat and leave nothing but bones. Later, if a herd passes near the sun-bleached bones, it will stop. Carefully, the elephants feel the bones, turn them over, and sometimes pick them up and carry them around.

Stories persist about elephant graveyards, places where old, sick, or injured animals go to die. The truth is that elephant bones can be found scattered over miles or piled together in one spot. A large collection of bones may mean it was the site of a mass killing by hunters or a place where elephants gathered and died together during a drought. In reality, old elephants die wherever their travels take them.

SUN-BLEACHED ELEPHANT BONES LIE SCATTERED ACROSS THE GRASSY PLAINS AT THE NGOROGORO CRATER.

5 Special Characteristics

> THE WONDERFUL ANIMAL IS LIKE A MOUNTAIN IN BULK AND STRENGTH, AND LIKE A LION IN COURAGE AND FEROCITY.
>
> —Mogul writer Abu Fazil, c. A.D. 1600

The elephants are restless; they sense the long dry spell is about to end. They have gathered at the one place they can still find some food and water. As a dark storm builds on the horizon, streaks of lightning light up the sky and plunge to the ground. Thunder rolls across the plains, and the first droplets of rain heighten the animals' anticipation. A fine drizzle soon turns into a downpour. The animals shiver, and their skin glistens as the rain deeply soaks them and everything else. In a few weeks, it will be a time of plenty as the grasses sprout anew. Then the

HOLDING ITS TRUNK UP LIKE A PERISCOPE, THIS ELEPHANT IS SNIFFING THE AIR TO PICK UP SCENTS.

migrating families will meet other families, and the greeting animals will engage in jubilant and expressive fellowship.

Social Behavior

In the last chapter, we saw that the family unit is the core of elephant life. Radiating out from it is a complex social system.

A family of elephants may have a close relationship with one or more other families. Researcher Cynthia Moss of the Amboseli Elephant Research Project in Kenya calls those families a bond group. She learned that, "families in the same bond group greet each other, show friendly behavior towards one another, and spend more time with each other than with other family units in the population." A bond group comprises twenty-five to thirty related elephants in two or three families.

Different bond groups that share a home range without having territorial disputes may belong to a larger group called a clan. All the clans, together with the adult males, make up a population of elephants. Population sizes vary greatly, from a few hundred elephants to several thousand.

Female elephants usually remain with their family unit for their entire lives, encircled by close relatives. Based on her age, each cow has a place and a role within the family. A high-ranking cow reinforces her position with body language. If challenged, she may abruptly raise her head, then slowly lower it. Or, in a stronger display, the cow may twist her head to one side and shake it back and forth so her ears slap against her face. The oldest mature female is always the leader. When she dies, the next oldest female, sometimes her daughter, takes her place.

Male calves stay with their birth family until they are teenagers, or until they feel confident enough to live apart from their mothers. Male calves mature at different rates. Generally, a male elephant is ready for independent living when he is fourteen, and he leaves then. But he will be chased away sooner if he shows sexual interest in the females.

A young bull may join other young males in small peer groups, or join with older males in bull groups, or he might decide to go solo. Within a bull group, a male's role and status are defined and adjusted by tests of strength. In this ritual fighting, the bulls raise their heads, clash tusks, shove each other, then hook their trunks as one tries to dominate the other. These trials almost always end without bloodshed. Throughout their lives, males alternate between joining bachelor herds or wandering alone. Very old bulls, massive creatures with enormous tusks, sometimes spend their last days in solitary retirement.

Elaborate Greetings

Few animals greet each other with as much enthusiasm as elephants. Whether it is a female reuniting with her family or the mingling of families in a bond group, elephants greet each other with noisy, affectionate commotion. Greeters entwine their trunks, raise their heads in the air, and click their tusks together. They roar, rumble, and trumpet noisily, all the while flapping their ears. The display often includes urinating and dropping dung, which imparts scent and helps re-establish relationships. Streams of liquid flow from the elephant's cheek glands, or temporal glands, a small opening between the eye and ear.

Sounds

The expressions of joy elephants show in greeting one another are part of their repertoire of at least twenty-five distinct vocal sounds. Each has a clear meaning. Elephants can roar mightily,

ELEPHANTS GREET ONE ANOTHER BY TOUCHING TRUNKS AND SNIFFING EACH
OTHER'S FACE AND BODY.

rumble softly, scream loudly, growl, and grunt. Trumpeting, the
most familiar sound, is shrill and ear-splitting. In addition to its
use in the greeting ritual, trumpeting also expresses surprise and
fear. For example, elephants have been known to trumpet if sur-
prised by predators or humans.

Since humans do not speak the same language as elephants,
researchers can only guess what the elephants are saying. Some

clues come from watching elephant behavior and their responses to the different calls.

Long-distance Calls

How do individuals and families scattered over miles of open grasslands or dense forests communicate with each other? First of all, elephants have a well-developed sense of hearing. It is so acute that they can hear calls from some distance away. And researchers have discovered that elephants use low-frequency calls, or infrasound, to send those messages over a distance of several miles. In 1984, researcher Katherine Payne watched Asian elephants at the Oregon Zoo in Portland, Oregon. She felt a "throbbing in the air" and figured out that the elephants were the source of the throbbing. Did they communicate using infrasound?

To find out, Ms. Payne recorded the vibrations the elephants made at the zoo. She discovered the animals were using a frequency range of 14 to 24 hertz, too low for humans to hear. Later, she and others continued the work in Etosha, Namibia. The semi-desert site offered good visibility to observe and record elephant behavior.

The researchers played back the calls they had recorded at Etosha. Then they videotaped the responses of elephant families at Etosha as they suddenly stood motionless for as long as a minute, trying to locate the source of the calls.

In one experiment, recordings of the intense, low-frequency calls that females make to advertise for a mate brought bulls to the scene. When other tape recordings were played, females and males raised their ears and listened intently. Males walked toward the loudspeakers. Females answered with calls of their own. Through these experiments, the scientists confirmed that elephants use infrasound to keep in touch with each other. Their calls are carried for at least 2.5 miles (4 km). The research helps explain how elephants communicate at night and in forests, or in high grass where their vision is blocked. It also explains how they know that a family member is in trouble. Constant communication through sounds strengthens the bonds that are the key to elephant survival.

ADULT FEMALE AFRICAN ELEPHANTS PLACE THEIR CALVES BETWEEN THEM FOR SAFETY.

Vision, Smell, and Touch

Elephants have good vision, but they rely more on their keen senses of smell and touch. An elephant's trunk is especially sensitive to both. Stretched up high in the air, like a periscope in a submarine, the trunk is able to pick up even faint odors. In that way, the animal detects ripe fruit in a far-off tree, a distant pool of water, and enemies. It has often been reported that elephants can smell a human being more than a mile (1.6 km) away.

At no time is smell more important than in mating. Bulls regularly sniff a female's urine to find out whether she is ready to mate. Or a bull may keep the tip of his trunk in a female's armpit, and at intervals, put it into his mouth. There, sensors called a Jacobson's organ can tell if she is ready to mate.

Touching with their trunks, elephants learn about their environment and their companions, and they develop strong family bonds. They sniff each other's face and body and put their trunk tip into each other's mouth, temporal glands, and ears. They stand head to head, trunk to trunk, in calm reassurance. Or, perhaps, they are engaged in quiet conversation.

Body Language

As with most animals, body language communicates a range of emotions and information. Humans may shake their heads or shrug their shoulders. Even without words, the meaning is clear. The same is true for elephants.

A relaxed and calm elephant lets its trunk hang down and its ears lay back. An excited elephant moves its ears forward and raises its head slightly. If the elephant wants to warn an intruder, it will stand tall to make itself look bigger. It will spread out its ears while it holds up its tusks and tail. To emphasize the threat even more, the elephant may shake its head, flap its ears, and take a few steps toward the intruder.

An angry elephant lets its intentions be known quickly. If the elephant plans to attack, rather than bluff, the trunk is pulled back safely to the chest, the ears flattened, and the head held down so the tusks are forward. Look out!

There are times when an elephant will display a submissive posture to a higher-ranking animal. To show respect for rank, it might back up or turn away, place its trunk in its mouth, or touch its temporal gland.

A YOUNG CALF LOOKS TO ITS MOTHER FOR PROTECTION, COMFORT, AND FOOD.

Intelligence and Memory

Is it true that elephants never forget? Elephants do have good memories, and some have better long-term memories than others. The matriarch remembers for years the routes to food and water in all seasons that she learned from her mother. Elephant families remember and readily greet distant relatives in their clan, even though they seldom see them. Elephants remember good and bad experiences and people for a long time. They react appropriately when they see the friend or enemy again.

Scientists believe the elephants' long-term memory may be linked to their very large brains. Not wanting to rely only on observed behavior, a few scientists have performed experiments to test their memory. In the 1950s, Drs. Bernard Rensch and Rudolf Altevogt of the Zoological Institute, University of Muenster, Germany, worked with an eight-year-old female Asian elephant. In experiments, the elephant was shown symbols similar to the drawings below. She learned to distinguish one pair from thirteen image pairs. With every correct answer, she got a treat as a reward. Once one task was learned, she was given additional pairs until all thirteen image pairs were memorized.

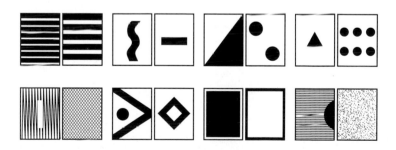

In later experiments, the number of pairs increased to twenty-six. After a year, she still remembered twenty-four of the twenty-six pairs. The researchers were so impressed that they expanded and varied the tests. Twenty pairs of patterns were presented to her in thirty variations for a total of six hundred selections. The elephant responded correctly most of the time.

Thirty-two years later, and without any contact with their pupil over those years, the researchers presented the now forty-year-old elephant with the original pairs of images. She did not recognize the symbols. However, she remembered the men and warmly touched and embraced them with her trunk. The fact that she remembered the scientists she hadn't seen for thirty-two years is itself extraordinary.

Working Elephants

For about five thousand years, Asian elephants have been trained and put to work, mostly in Southeast Asia. Elephants felled trees and carried heavy logs. No animal, not even a horse, is as well equipped to help humans. The elephant's trunk grips, lifts, and holds a tree while the tusks support and raise up heavy logs. Its body is agile yet powerful. Treated well, elephants respond well. Bulls and cows are used as working elephants. In spite of problems during musth, bull elephants are often preferred for logging because they are bigger and stronger.

After wild elephants are captured, calmed, and tamed, they go to elephant school. Each elephant usually has one trainer, or mahout, for its entire life. He is the person the elephant learns to obey, and eventually they develop a strong bond. Training begins with the basics, and a skilled elephant serves as tutor. Student elephants learn commands, like lifting a foot or getting down on their knees. When the student copies the actions of the tutor correctly, it is rewarded with kind words, pats, and tasty morsels. Generally, the student elephant learns thirty or more easy commands in six months. A spiked stick called an elephant hook, or ankus, is sometimes used to control an elephant and to

TRAINED ELEPHANTS HAVE PERFORMED AND ENTERTAINED IN CIRCUSES SINCE THE DAYS OF ANCIENT ROME.

encourage it to follow instructions. A good mahout only needs to lightly press the ankus to guide the elephant and would never draw blood.

After basic training, the elephant must get used to the feel of a harness and learn more commands for the hard work ahead. The student learns about sixty new spoken commands in addition to specific signals the mahout gives by pressing his feet behind the elephant's ears. It takes two to three years before the elephant is ready to work. Elephants continue to be taught in this way because humans find them to be intelligent, dutiful, and good-natured students.

Circus Performers

Those same traits make elephants ideal pupils for circus trainers. They build on the elephant's natural abilities and behaviors to teach them tricks. A headstand, for instance, is a position an elephant may use when digging for minerals in the wild. Elephants can be taught to walk upright on their hind legs, balance skillfully on a table or a huge ball, and even ride a bicycle. Many of the tricks put great strain on their knee joints and backs, however, causing the animals pain. Forcing elephants to perform extreme tricks is cruel. Today many circus companies are setting a better example with modest acts.

Unlike Asian working elephants, circus performers spend long hours tied up on a short chain in a tent stall or travel trailer.

A CIRCUS ELEPHANT GETS ITS TOENAILS PAINTED BEFORE GOING INTO THE RING IN THIS 1942 PHOTOGRAPH.

MANY ELEPHANTS PERFORM FOR A CROWD.

They suffer from boredom and anxiety. Some circuses are trying to improve this situation. The Swiss circus Knie provides its elephants with roomy stalls and outdoor space to move around in. Animal trainers also believe that elephants benefit from the mental stimulation and good exercise of training. Nevertheless, trainers must be constantly alert to any signs of stress or anger in their animals. Elephants' natural good nature can easily be crushed in captivity.

Elephants, especially big bulls, are unpredictable and can be dangerous. Elephants are naturally gentle, but pent-up frustrations can cause them to strike out in rage. The list of people killed or injured by angry or frightened elephants is long.

Today, the number of circus elephants in North America is less than 250. Many people are beginning to question whether these intelligent, social giants belong in circuses. Should we confine them to an unnatural life for our enjoyment?

6 The Cycle of Life

THE BABY ELEPHANT'S TRUNK IS ITS MAIN CONTACT WITH
THE WORLD AROUND IT. A BABY OFTEN STANDS VIGOROUSLY
SWINGING ITS TRUNK BACK AND FORTH, TOSSING IT UP AND
DOWN, AND SOMETIMES WHIRLING IT AROUND IN A CIRCLE.

—Cynthia Moss, founder,
Amboseli Elephant Research Project, Kenya

As the dawn creeps above the horizon, a baby elephant
enters the world. She lies on the ground, kicking at the
birth sac that partially covers her body. Her mother and older
sister stand next to her and tear away the sac with their tusks.
Then, wrapping their trunks around the tiny elephant's body,
they gently coax her to get up. The newborn's little legs stretch
out. She struggles to stand, yet each time she does, she falls back
down to the ground. She tries again and again. Her little legs
wobble, but she is determined. Swaying back and forth, the calf

NOT KNOWING HOW TO USE ITS TRUNK YET, A BABY
ELEPHANT BENDS DOWN TO EAT GRASS WITH ITS MOUTH.

works to keep her balance. When success is hers at last, she takes a few tentative steps and reaches her mother's side. Mother and baby touch and smell each other with their trunks. The newborn seeks her mother's breast and suckles with her mouth.

Other family members arrive and greet the mother, stretching their trunks to her mouth. They gently touch the small calf to

A MOTHER ELEPHANT FREQUENTLY TOUCHES HER NEWBORN CALF WITH HER TRUNK IN ORDER TO REASSURE IT.

welcome her into the family. If all goes well, the youngster will have a long life ahead, surrounded by a nurturing family.

The Mating Game

Mating can take place throughout the year, but it generally occurs in the rainy season, when there is a ready supply of protein-rich grasses. This helps ensure that a pregnant cow gets enough to eat. Bulls and cows must find each other and court before mating. To do so, they advertise by scent and sound their readiness and willingness to get together.

Healthy female elephants usually reach sexual maturity between seven and twelve years old. That is when the young cow begins her estrous cycle, or period of sexual receptivity. Estrus, the time when the cow is capable of conceiving, lasts two to six days. If she does not conceive during that time, estrus recurs in two months. The female sends out low-frequency calls to announce her sexual state so that males will be attracted to her. The scent of her urine also tells visiting bulls of her condition.

Bulls also reach sexual maturity before they are fourteen, but they usually do not mate for many years. Mature bulls – those over thirty-five—mate the most often. They aggressively chase younger bulls away. According to researcher Cynthia Moss, "The older a male is, the more successful he is in mating with as many females as possible."

In the wild, adult males over twenty-five start to come into a condition called musth or must. It is a period of intense sexual activity and increased aggression. By the time a bull is forty, his musth cycle will last three to four months of the year. During that time, he continually searches for cows in estrus.

During musth, a bull's temporal glands swell and excrete great amounts of a dark, oily, strong-smelling matter. It runs down the bull's face and leaves dark stains. He uses this excretion to advertise his condition, rubbing his forehead, cheeks, and trunk against trees, leaving a strong scent.

A bull in musth is unpredictable and combative. Zoologist Joyce Poole discovered that a bull in musth has four times the normal amount of the male hormone called testosterone, which is believed to play a part in the aggressive behavior of many mammals, including humans.

A bull in musth is always dominant over a bull that is not in musth, regardless of its age and size. He is ready, not only to guard a cow in estrus, but also to fight for the right to mate with her. Long, serious contests sometimes occur between bulls if they are similar in age and size. Unlike the practice sparring in bachelor herds, these bulls clash furiously as each tries to throw the other to the ground. Sometimes one bull ends up badly wounded or even killed by the other's tusks.

Courtship can be lengthy. It involves mutual touching of mouths, temporal glands, and sex organs. The pair twine trunks and rumble softly. The cow may press her backside against the bull's head as he places his trunk along her body. If she is not ready, as often happens, she bolts and runs away, bowing her head and swinging her trunk and tail. The bull follows in hot pursuit. She comes back toward him. They meet head to head and repeat the rituals. When she finally stands still, he jumps up to stand behind her and lays his trunk over her neck and head. His hind legs support his great weight. The mating act is short, lasting only ten or fifteen seconds. The other elephants may gather around to watch and perhaps enjoy the spectacle. Cynthia Moss witnessed such a scene in Amboseli National Park, Kenya. An entire elephant family celebrated the occasion of mating with trumpeting, rumbling, and roaring. Moss speculated that they were "broadcasting the news far and wide."

As long as the cow is in estrus, she will accept the bull, but they do not form a lifelong bond. After they part, the cow rejoins her family. The bull may continue his quest for other females or return to a bachelor life.

Birth and Babies

Gestation, the time needed for a baby to develop in its mother's womb, is twenty-one to twenty-two months for elephants. That is about a year longer than it takes for human babies to develop. The cow usually gives birth in a semi-squatting position. Her mother or her sister stays close to protect her as well as to assist and soothe her during the birth. Sometimes the family group forms a circle around the pregnant cow to protect her during the delivery, when she is most vulnerable to predators.

After waves of contractions and steady pushing, the baby elephant's hindquarters appear, and in seconds the calf drops to the ground. Most often it is a single calf; in rare cases, twins. The mother turns to sniff her newborn with her trunk. With the help of other females, she frees the calf from the sticky amniotic sac, and the newborn begins to move around and tries to stand. At the same time, the cow delivers the afterbirth, the organ that fed and protected the baby in the womb. The mother eats the afterbirth for its nutrients and to discourage predators from approaching.

Asian elephant calves weigh between 132 and 253 pounds (60–115 kg.). African calves are a little heavier, weighing 198 to 297 pounds (90–135 kg). Male calves weigh more than females. Both are about 3 feet (95 cm) tall. Newborns are quite hairy. Soft, thick brown hair covers their bodies and the tops of their head. The hair falls out after a few months. A calf's ears are pinkish for the first two weeks of its life.

Within an hour of birth, the calf manages to stand up and

seeks its mother's nipples. Cows have two teats between their front legs. The calf stretches its body up to reach them, then uses its mouth to suck. Since the calf does not need the trunk to suckle, it is curled over its head and out of the way.

For the first months of its life, the calf lives mainly on its mother's milk. She lets the calf suckle on demand, often small amounts several times an hour. Elephant milk is very high in fat and protein, and the baby puts on weight very quickly.

At first, the newborn stays close by its mother or stands between her legs. The calf frequently nurses or reaches out to smell and touch her for reassurance. She guides with the gentle

CALVES CONTINUE TO SUCKLE MILK FROM THEIR MOTHERS FOR TWO TO FOUR YEARS.

A BABY ELEPHANT HOLDS ITS MOTHER'S TAIL, SO THEY CANNOT GET SEPARATED.

comforting touch of her trunk, making sure her youngster is out of harm's way. In Asia, young calves can be easy targets for tigers, while in Africa, hyenas or lions may lie in wait.

Occasionally, a cow with a young calf dies. Without its mother's milk and care, the calf will die too, unless it is adopted by another cow who is nursing young. But that does not always happen.

Childhood

For elephants, as with humans, childhood lasts for years, and there is much for the young animals to learn. Elephant calves grow up in the protective care of a loving, nurturing matriarchal family. Sisters, aunts, and grandmothers help raise and train the young. The successful rearing of calves to maturity ensures the survival of the family unit and the elephants in general.

Juvenile females, called allomothers or aunties, are attracted to young calves. They play an important role in their upbringing. An allomother stands alongside the calf's mother to provide shade for the sleeping baby. She stays behind to make sure the calves safely leave the bathing site and follow the family. And if a calf wanders off or gets stuck in the mud, the allomother rushes to its side at its first cries of distress.

In this way, the allomothers give the mother more time to feed and rest so she is sure to produce enough milk. At the same time, the young females get practice for the time when they will have calves of their own.

For the first months, though, the newborn clings to its mother and relies on her for everything. The mother introduces her frightened calf to the watering hole. She showers it with water to cool off and later may spray dust over it to keep insects away. Even as it grows stronger and older, the calf continues to nurse for at least two to four years.

After a few months, the calf tries eating plants. It gets down on its knees and munches grasses with its mouth or chews leaves from low-growing bushes. Putting its trunk into its mother's mouth is also an easy way to find food.

Before it can feed itself easily, though, the calf has to learn to control its trunk. A young elephant's trunk looks and acts like a floppy rubber hose. It takes practice, practice, and more practice

A YOUNG CALF HAS TO STRETCH UPWARD TO REACH ITS MOTHER'S NIPPLES, WHICH ARE LOCATED BETWEEN HER FRONT LEGS.

to get the hang of using it. The calf begins by reaching out and touching everything. Grabbing a small twig lying on the ground or picking up a bunch of grass is a challenge. With enough repetition, the calf becomes more skilled at using its trunk like a hand. Baby elephants sometimes suck on the fingers of their

trunks, just as human babies suck their thumbs. Drinking requires a bit more work. At first, more water spills than goes into the mouth. By three years of age, the calf has usually mastered the art of drinking, and only a few drops dribble onto the ground.

By the age of three to four weeks, the young calf leaves its mother's protection and seeks playmates. Calves spend a good part of the day playing. They love to run through tall grasses, chasing and charging each other. And any elephant in the family that lies down offers an irresistible invitation to play. The baby

THE CALF'S OPEN MOUTH PROVIDES A GLIMPSE OF ITS FIRST MOLARS.

elephants climb onto the head and back of the elephant that is on the ground and squeal with delight as they slide off.

Play strengthens the bonds between family members. Play fighting, especially among males, helps to determine who is strongest and most likely to remain so when they leave the fam ily group.

7 Conservation

> WHAT LAND IS SAVED FOR THE ELEPHANT IS SAVED FOR EVERY ANIMAL THAT LIVES THERE.
>
> —Cynthia Moss, founder,
> Amboseli Elephant Research Project, Kenya

Gathering under large shade trees, the elephants relax, and nod off to sleep. Nearby, but unnoticed, poachers creep close to the sleeping animals. Suddenly, the men open fire. For a terrifying few minutes, their automatic weapons blaze. The elephants sink to their knees or stagger a few feet before collapsing. The guns stop, and it is quiet. All the animals lie dead on the ground. The poachers act quickly. With chainsaws and axes, they cut away most of each animal's skull to remove the heavy tusks. The prized ivory is swiftly carried away.

White Gold

For an elephant, ivory tusks are tools and weapons. For humans, ivory is almost priceless, highly valued and traded for many centuries. Ivory is sometimes called "white gold" because

RANGERS DISPLAY TWO LARGE IVORY TUSKS.

IVORY HAS BEEN TRADED FOR CENTURIES.

it is so precious. Beautiful, cool, and smooth, it is easily carved and long lasting. Elaborate designs may be carefully carved into the white tusks, and, after polishing, the ivory takes on a softly glowing luster. It is no wonder that the demand for ivory has grown steadily.

Ivory statuettes rested in the tombs of ancient Egyptian kings. Wealthy Romans at the time of Caesar (49 to 44 B.C.) sought luxury items such as ivory jewelry and statues. In later centuries, carvings became more detailed and costly. On each continent, ivory artisans prospered. Ivory carvings are among the works of art in European churches and palaces. Indian craftsmen excelled at combining ivory and wood in an intricate veneer to adorn furniture and other objects. In Japan, the popularity of ivory *hanko*, signature seals, and *netsuke*, miniature sculptures, made Japan one of the world's biggest consumers of ivory.

As trade in ivory flourished, African elephants were not safe from poachers, even in national parks. Their numbers declined greatly. It is estimated that 10 million elephants lived in Africa in 1900. By 1979, the population had dropped to 1.3 million. Ten years later, only half survived.

Human greed speeded up the slaughter. The price of ivory rose from $5.50 per two pounds (1 kg) in the 1960s, to $50 for the same amount in the late 1970s, and up to $200 to $300 by the late 1980s. Some 600 to 1,000 tons of ivory were sold every year, and most came from poaching. Concerns rose. Americans launched a "Save the Elephant: Don't Buy Ivory" campaign. African nations tried to control poaching, but, in some areas, organized gangs devastated once abundant herds. For example, poachers in Kenya killed 1,000 elephants in 1988. The gangs typically got $6 a pound (0.5 kg) for tusks. In one night, they might earn $100. That is a lot of money in countries where, on average, a worker earns about $20 a month.

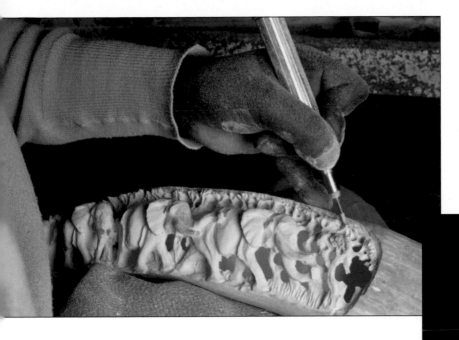

AN ARTISAN USES A SMALL DRILL TO CARVE THE FIGURES OF ELEPHANTS INTO A PIECE OF IVORY.

IVORY HAS BEEN CARVED INTO MANY KINDS OF SCULPTURE AND OTHER OBJECTS, SUCH AS BILLIARD BALLS, VENEER ON WHITE PIANO KEYS, TOURIST SOUVENIRS, AND SIGNATURE SEALS.

The world rallied around the elephants' cause. At the height of poaching, Kenyan president Daniel Arap Moi burned 13 tons of confiscated poached ivory in a huge symbolic bonfire. His message to the rest of the world: Stop buying ivory.

In 1989, the Convention on International Trade in Endangered Species of Wild Fauna and Flora (CITES) banned all trade in ivory and other elephant products, such as hides. Some African countries did not support the ban. South Africa, Botswana, and Zimbabwe already had instituted strong protective measures and were less affected by poaching. Zimbabwe urged the conservation and management of wildlife as an alternative to an ivory ban.

The poachers' guns fell silent as the price of ivory fell. The decline of African elephants slowed, and the population is growing again. Even so, as long as there is a demand for ivory and it is profitable, illegal hunting will exist.

In 1999, CITES relaxed the rules and allowed the countries of Botswana, Namibia, and Zimbabwe to sell stockpiled ivory. No ivory from poached elephants was sold. And all profits from the sales were to be used to protect elephant herds.

Asian Elephants—Their Story

The range and population of Asian elephants have been slowly eroding over centuries. Historians tell us that 5,000 years ago Asian elephants could be found in Syria and Iraq, east across Asia south of the Himalayas, in the Southeast Asian and Malay peninsulas, and north into China. Their numbers were vast.

Today, *Elephas maximus* is classified as an endangered species, in danger of extinction. No more than 35,000 to 56,000 of these elephants remain. They have disappeared from China and western Asia. Their slow decline came as a result of human actions.

The Asian elephant culture began in the Indus River Valley, present day Pakistan, where Asian elephants were first captured. The Indus people tamed and trained the giants for field and forest work and for warfare. Ivory was also prized in Asia, and big bulls with large tusks were targeted. Later, elephant herds filled the stables of wealthy princes and kings. The elephant masters found it was easier and less expensive to capture the animals than to breed them. Sometimes as many as 400 elephants were rounded up in a single drive. Many of them did not survive the brutal breaking-in process.

Today, as in the past, human populations continue to expand throughout Asia. Fertile valleys are cleared for agriculture and settlements, and forests are cut for firewood and lumber. Mining and the construction of roads and dams destroy land while crowding elephants into smaller spaces.

Elephants in Sri Lanka

The story of elephants in Ceylon, now the Republic of Sri Lanka, is one of continual pressure from humans. It illustrates why Asian elephants are close to extinction. For centuries, the Ceylonese captured elephants to be used as work animals and to export to other Asian countries. Still, 200 years ago, more than 18,000 elephants occupied the island's forests.

In 1796, Britain took control of the island and began clearing the forests and driving out the elephants. Coffee, tea, and rubber plantations replaced those forests. Problems began when the elephants returned to their former feeding lands. They inflicted heavy damage to the plantations, and the owners responded with a massive trapping and hunting campaign. One infamous elephant hunter, Major Thomas W. Rogers, single-handedly killed 1,400 elephants. And there were many elephant hunters. At the same time, elephants continued to be captured to supply an elephant work force.

When Ceylon became the Republic of Sri Lanka in 1972, even more forests and lands were opened up for development. The forests were replaced by acres of rice and sugar cane. Human settlements followed. As they grew, the elephant population decreased. Fewer than 2,000 elephants are left in Sri Lanka today, and there is growing worry about saving those that remain. New national parks have been created and existing ones expanded to give the elephants more feeding grounds.

TOURISTS IN NATIONAL PARKS CAN SEE WILD ELEPHANTS FROM THE SAFETY OF THEIR AUTOMOBILES.

Parks and Reserves

Parks and reserves, safe havens dedicated to preserving wildlife, are scattered throughout Africa and Southeast Asia. Hunting is forbidden. In some parks, trained and fully armed game wardens watch over the wildlife and patrol the borders to prevent poaching. Elephants safely thrive and multiply for a while. But confined, isolated, and unable to migrate to new feeding areas, they soon eat all there is. Their existence becomes threatened.

In South Africa and neighboring countries, elephant populations are managed to maintain the balance between them and available plants. Culling, or legal killing, is conducted. A government unit shoots an entire elephant family at one time. The animals are butchered, and nothing wasted. Money from the sale of the ivory, meat, and hides supports conservation in the parks.

Culling is not only controversial, but some people see it as a crime to kill these intelligent creatures. Many conservationists believe the problem is not too many elephants, but too little land. Yet land is scarce everywhere. One possible answer lies in extending fragmented parks and reserves with the use of corridors, or connecting strips of land. Elephants, as well as other

A TUSK IS PULLED AWAY FROM THE CARCASS OF A POACHED ELEPHANT.

FARMERS PUT UP FENCES
TO KEEP ELEPHANTS AWAY
FROM THEIR CROPS. SOME-
TIMES, ELEPHANTS USE
THEIR TUSKS AND BODIES
TO BREAK THE WIRES TO
REACH THE FOOD.

wildlife, can freely follow the rains and growing seasons by traveling along the corridors. Developing corridors is a challenge,
however, because the land surrounding parks may be privately
owned farms or ranches or public roads.

In Sri Lanka, a strip of land connects two widely separated
parks so elephants may move easily between them. Bordering
Nepal and India, the Terai Arc region is an area of 12,000 square
miles (31,200 km²). It is a land of forests and grasslands with
many large mammals, including elephants, tigers and rhinocer-
oses. And more than 2 million people also depend on the land's

natural resources for their livelihood. Its eleven protected areas remain isolated from one another. A challenging ten-year plan involves reconnecting them into one secure habitat. Local people are the key to the plan's success. They will be encouraged to plant trees, such as teak, that will provide a good income for them later. Villagers will be encouraged to manage the land correctly and will be trained to do so.

Human Population Explosion

Even if hunting ceased today, elephants would continue to be vulnerable. People and land development provide the greatest threats to the elephant's long-term survival. In some Asian and

AN ASIAN ELEPHANT GRAZES ALONGSIDE A BRUSHFIRE.

African countries, human populations double every thirty to forty years. Natural habitats shrink as humans settle them and build housing. The result is less living space for elephants and other animals. Their migration routes are disrupted. Sometimes, animals become concentrated in remote scattered pockets of vegetation, or in national parks and reserves. Often, farms surround those places. Cattle may graze in reserves and compete with wildlife for grass.

Elephants confined to small spaces or marginal lands with less vegetation soon eat all the available food. Hunger makes them move away, and they often return to their old feeding grounds. What they find, though, are farms, houses, and grazing cattle. It is disastrous for everyone. A family of elephants can devour a crop of corn, sugar cane, or bananas very quickly. They may knock down trees or destroy homes to reach food. For the Asian or African farmer, it means no harvest and a hungry family. Clashes are increasing.

Farmers try clanging bells and beating drums to drive away the hungry elephants. They will kill elephants to protect their farms. Just as often, though, bold elephants attack and injure or kill humans and their domestic animals. In some places, electric fencing and wide ditches have been installed to stop the elephants.

But at a few ranches in southern Africa, fences are coming down and wildlife is free to wander. The ranchers have found that they make more money from managing sport hunting or photography safaris than from raising cattle.

Educating people who live with wildlife is essential. Local people must also be given a voice in the management of wildlife because it is their resource. People have a greater stake in protecting wildlife and habitat when they are involved. Farmers and ranchers must be compensated for damages and attacks by elephants. The marketing of ivory substitutes, such as plastics, resins,

and palm nuts, may help reduce the demand for ivory.

Conservationists believe that long-term solutions are needed to benefit both people and elephants. How can land, food, and water be effectively shared between elephants and humans? There are no easy answers. Each country or region must decide how best to save elephants and help people.

The situation for humans and elephants changes almost daily as climate, natural disasters, wars, and disease affect everyone. Conserving these magnificent pachyderms is a challenge, not a burden. It is up to us to make sure elephants survive for many generations to come.

Glossary

allomother—a female elephant that helps the mother elephant care for her calf

amniotic sac—the membrane surrounding the embryo

browse—to feed on leaves, berries, or twigs

Buddha—an Indian religious leader who lived between 563 and 483 B.C.

Buddhism—a religion based on the teachings of Buddha

cementum—a bonelike substance that covers the outer surface of a tooth's root

crevasse—a deep split in glacial ice

culling—the legal killing of elephants to reduce their population

dentin—a hard substance that makes up the main part of a tooth

drought—a long period of dry weather

estrus—the time period during which a female mammal can get pregnant

enamel—the hard outer layer of teeth

fossil—the remains or traces of an organism

gestation—the period of development before birth, or pregnancy

graze—to feed on growing grass

herbivore—an animal that eats only plants

herd—a large group of animals

Hinduism—a religion, philosophy, and social system that originated in India

infrasound—very low sounds, below the range humans can hear

ivory—smooth, hard, white incisor teeth or tusks

mahout—the Indian word for a person who is the keeper and trainer of an elephant

mammal—an animal that is warm blooded, has a backbone, has hair, and produces milk to feed its offspring

mammoth—a large, extinct elephant that had a woolly coat

mastodon—a prehistoric elephantlike animal that lived in North America and died out about 10,000 years ago

matriarch—the mature, adult female leader of an elephant family

megaherbivore—a huge plant-eating mammal

Moeritherium—a very early elephant with traces of small tusks and a trunk

molar—a tooth with a broad chewing surface

musth—an annual period when bulls become aggressive, pick fights with other bulls, and search for females who are ready to mate

niche—the place and role of a species in a biological community

pachyderms—large, thick-skinned, hoofed mammals, like the elephant, rhinoceros, and hippopotamus

permafrost—permanently frozen earth

poacher—a person who hunts illegally

population—all the animals living in a specific place

predator—an animal that hunts other animals

prehistory—the period before people began to write down events

Probiscideans—large, long-nosed mammals belonging to the scientific order Proboscidea

proboscis—a long flexible nose or trunk

protozoan—a one-celled organism

savanna—flat grassland with scattered shrubs and trees

species—a group of plants or animals that share similar characteristics, can mate, and have fertile offspring

temporal gland—a small opening between the elephant's eye and ear from which thick secretions flow

ungulate—a hoofed mammal

African and Asian Elephants Species Checklist

All plants and animals have scientific names, which are written in Latin and are italicized. Some species also have common names. A scientific name begins with the genus, or first name, and is always capitalized. It is followed by the species and subspecies, which are written in lowercase.

Common names are written in lowercase unless the name comes from a proper noun. The common names for the species and subspecies of elephants generally describe where they live. Their scientific and common names are listed below.

Family: Elephantidae (elephants)

Loxodonta africana (African elephant)
Loxodonta africana africana (savanna elephant)
Loxodonta africana cyclotes (forest elephant)

Elephas maximus (Asian elephant)
Elephas maximus maximus (Ceylon elephant)
Elephas maximus hirsutus (Malaysian elephant)
Elephas maximus bengalensi (Indian elephant)
Elephas maximus sumatranus (Sumatran elephant)

African and Asian Elephants

	African Elephant	Asian (Indian) Elephant
Scientific Name	**Loxodonta africana**	**Elephas maximus**
Weight	Bulls up to 15,000 lbs (6,750 kg), Cows about 7,000 lbs (3,178 kg)	Bulls up to 9,400 lbs (4,268 kg), Cows to about 6,600 lbs (3,000 kg)
Height at shoulder	Bulls, 7–12 feet (2.2–3.7 m), Cows, up to 9 feet (2.8 m)	Bulls, 7.5–9 ft (2.4–2.9 m), Cows, 8 ft (2.4 m)
Features	Very large ears; tusks (both sexes); bulls have longer and heavier tusks; trunk tip has two grasping "fingers"	Tusks in most bulls, though some males have none; domed forehead; small ears do not cover shoulders; one "finger" in trunk tip
Reproduction	Gestation 22 months; usually one calf of 198–297 lbs (90–135 kg)	Gestation 22 months; usually one calf of 132–253 lbs (60–115 kg)
Life Cycle	Sexual maturity at 8–12 years; lives 50–70 years in the wild	Sexual maturity at 7–11 years; lives up to 69 years in captivity and about 40 in the wild
Food	Grasses, leaves, branches, fruits, roots, bark	Grasses, leaves, palm fronds, fruits
Habitat	Grasslands, marshes, woodlands, semi-deserts, forests of Africa	Jungles, open grasslands, marshes, and clearings of southern and southeastern Asia
Enemies	Humans; lions, hyenas, wild dogs, and crocodiles prey on young calves	Humans; tigers hunt young calves
Status	Threatened with extinction by hunting and habitat destruction; estimated population: 600,000	Threatened with extinction; fewer than 50,000 in the wild

Further Research

If you are interested in knowing more about elephants, here are books, magazines, videos, web sites, and organizations that will be of help.

Books and Magazines for Young People

Encyclopedia of Mammals, New York: Marshall Cavendish, 1997.

Moss, Cynthia, and Martyn Colbeck. *Echo of the Elephants*. New York: William Morrow and Company, 1992.

Payne, Katherine. "Elephant Talk," *National Geographic*, vol. 176, no. 2, August 1989.

Redmond, Ian. *Eyewitness Books: Elephant*. New York: Dorling Kindersley Ltd., 1993.

Taylor, Barbara. *Nature Watch: Elephants*. New York: Lorenz Books, 1993.

Videos

Elephant. 1994 BBC Wildvision

Reflections on Elephants. 1994 National Geographic Video

Survivors of the Skeleton Coast. 1993 National Geographic Video

The Urban Elephant, 2000 Nature Video

Bibliography

These books and magazines were some of the material used by the author while researching this book. They offer more detailed information on an adult level.

Alden, Pete C., Richard D. Estes, Duane Schlitter, and Bunny McBride. *National Audubon Society Field Guide to African Wildlife*. New York: Alfred A. Knopf,1998.

Chadwick, Douglas H. "Out of Space, Out of Time Elephants." *National Geographic*, vol.179, no. 5, May 1991.

Douglas-Hamilton, Iain and Oria. *Among the Elephants*. New York: Viking Press, 1975.

Gröning, Karl. *Elephants, A Cultural and Natural History*. Cologne, Germany: Könemann,1998.

Johnson, Kirk R., and Richard K. Stuckey. *Prehistoric Journey: A History of Life on Earth*. Boulder, CO: Rinehart Publishers, 1995.

Moss, Cynthia, and Martyn Colbeck. *Echo of the Elephants*. New York: William Morrow and Company, 1992.

Parker, Sybil, ed. *"Gryimek" Encyclopedia of Mammals*, vol. 4. New York: McGraw-Hill, 1990.

Payne, Katherine. "Elephant Talk." *National Geographic*, vol. 176, no. 2, August 1989.

Scullard, H.H. *The Elephant in the Greek and Roman World*. New York: Cornell University Press, 1974.

Vesilind, Priit J. "Monsoons." *National Geographic*, vol. 166, no.6, December 1984.

Web Sites

http://www.african-edventure.org
> Travel and meet the wildlife, including elephants, on Edventure through Africa.

http://www.oregonzoo.org
> The Oregon Zoo site provides fact sheets on and photographs of Asian elephants.

http://elephant.elehost.com
> A site with lots of information about elephants.

http://www.livingwithelephants.org
> A nonprofit organization in Botswana, Africa, which explores the relationship between the African elephant and people.

http://www.nationalgeographic.kids/creature_feature/0103/elephants2_html
> Describes elephants and how they live.

http://www.naturehaven.com/elephant.html
> General information and news about elephants.

http://www.natzoo.si.edu
> The Smithsonian National Zoological Park has an Elephant House that features Asian elephants. Photos and videos of the elephants' activities are offered at the site. Find out also about Kandula, the male Asian elephant calf, born at the zoo in November 2001.

http://www.nczooeletrack.org
> The North Carolina Zoological Park web site features the elephant's place in the culture of Northern Cameroon, Africa.

http://www.oaba.org/animals.htm
> Outdoor Amusement Business Association provides the business point of view on maintaining circuses.

http://www.ozemail.com.au/~cannont
> Stories of the elephants of Sri Lanka.

http://www.pbs.org/wnet/nature/elephants
> Information about African elephants, including their special characteristics, and the poaching problem.

http://www.save-the-elephants.org
> A conservation organization that focuses on research, education, grassroots conservation, monitoring, and protection of elephants.

http://www.elephant.tnet.co.th
> Information about the Friends of the Asian Elephant Foundation. Volunteers provide medical treatment for numbers of sick and abused elephants, so they may be returned to their natural habitat in Thailand.

Organizations that Support Conservation

African Wildlife Foundation
1400 16th Street, NW, Suite 120
Washington, DC 20036
http://www.awf.org

Wildlife Conservation Society
> (formerly the New York Zoological Society)
185th Street and Southern Boulevard
Bronx, NY 10460
http://www.wcs.org

World Wildlife Fund
1250 24th Street, NW
Washington, DC 20037
http://www.worldwildlife.org

Index

Page numbers for illustrations are in **boldface**.

About the Author

GLORIA G. SCHLAEPFER shares her respect for the natural world through her writing, photography, and community activism. She has co-authored five books for children: *The African Rhinos*, *The Coyote*, *Pythons and Boas*, *Bats,* and, most recently, *Cheetahs*. Ms. Schlaepfer, who lives in Fullerton, California, has four children and four grandchildren.